A DAY IN THE LIFE

THE FANS
of Memorial Stadium

Joe Starita ~ Tom Tidball

Thanks to the University of Nebraska, Lincoln and the following companies for their generosity in producing this book:

Ameritas Life Insurance Company
First Federal Lincoln Bank
Jacob North Printing Company
Misty's Restaurant and Lounge
Nebraska Bookstore
Orent Graphics

For information write to: Tidball Productions ~ P.O. Box 6473 ~ Lincoln, NE 68506

ISBN: 0-9648992-2-1

Published and distributed by:
Nebraska Book Publishing Company
1300 Q Street ~ Lincoln, Nebraska 68508
Phone: 800-627-0027
             402-476-7755
Fax: 402-476-0111
E-Mail: nbookstore@aol.com

A DAY IN THE LIFE

THE FANS
of Memorial Stadium

Joe Starita ~ Tom Tidball

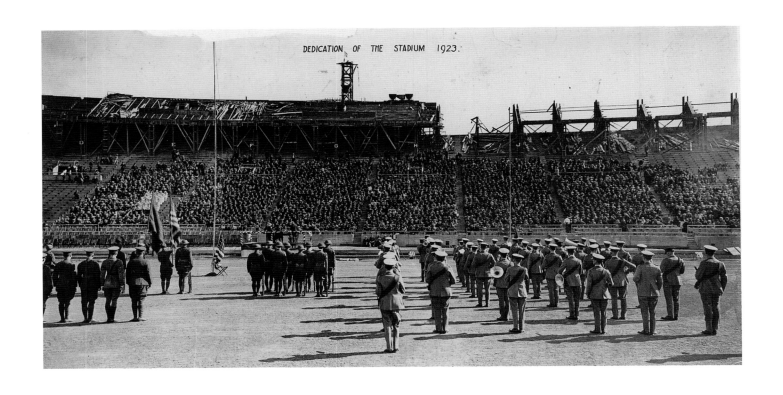

DEDICATION OF THE STADIUM 1923.

To the people of the plains who have endured depressions and world wars,

whose children remember the old Knot Hole Section and losing seasons,

whose grandchildren now march to the beat of tunnel music and national champions,

to all the fans who have made the journey and filled the stadium for every home game

in every autumn since 1962.

This book is for you.

Prologue

It is early September.

Another scorching summer slowly begins to fade on the Central Plains and there is the hint now of a new season, of a new rhythm to the life and the land. The children are returning to school, burnished faces and fresh haircuts. They wear new sneakers and crisp jeans, carry clean notepads in colorful backpacks. Soccer practice, piano lessons, cross country meets. Car pools and crowded calendars. Getting the bathroom is a little more competitive. Out back, the vegetable gardens are mostly barren — beets, tomatoes and cucumbers plucked from the vine and pulled from the earth, sealed in jars, ready for the colder months ahead. Beyond Main, beyond the edge of town, it is time, too, for the fields to yield their annual bounty of wheat and corn, soybeans and sorghum. Combines and harvesters work all day, into the night, and there is a growing line of trucks queuing up at the tall grain co-ops sprouting along the flat railroad tracks by the straight highways near shallow rivers. Soon, lawnmowers will give way to rakes, T-shirts to jackets, frivolity to homework. Longer days to longer nights. Green and brown to red and white. All around, the feel of fall is in the air.

There is something else in the air, too.

It has been discussed and debated for months, rolled over and played out in the corporate offices of Union Pacific and Mutual of Omaha, in the taverns and grange halls clustered along the Platte River Valley. At feed lots and sale barns throughout the Central Sandhills and in corridors and lobbies of the state Capitol. Feverish talk in the

hardware stores of the western high plains. At coffee shops and pool halls in the Pine Ridge country. In truck stops and motels flanking Interstate 80. At family restaurants, pharmacies and Pump and Pantries. From the Republican to the Loup to the Big Blue:

Who will start at quarterback?

Will the offensive line be as good as last year's?

What do you make of the defense?

Can they go all the way?

Got any extra tickets?

Tomorrow is the home opener. The first game of the season for the University of Nebraska football team.

The first game of the new season for their fans.

In the world of collegiate athletics, there are fans. And then there are those who follow Nebraska football. Two distinct, discernible species. Mutually exclusive. Separate and unequal. To wit: Other fans attend games and take an interest in their team. Nebraska fans sell out stadiums and follow their team with a loyalty, passion and endurance perhaps unrivaled in American sports.

And on this September Friday, their game plan is resolute, as ritualized as the spring planting and fall harvest. Some will come from Kansas and Colorado. Others from Iowa, Missouri and Wyoming. From California, New Mexico, Arizona and the Dakotas. But, mostly, they will come from Nebraska. Laden with sandwiches and soda, kids and pets, pennants, flags and banners, portable grills and portable radios, blankets, coolers, a thermos of coffee and tickets, they will pile into station wagons, sedans, campers, trucks, pickups, buses, jeeps, four-wheel drives and RVs, flowing from all corners of the state, tributaries of red meandering across the fall countryside, past downtown office buildings and suburban shopping malls, past fields of corn and wheat, past feed lots and the Pony Express route, cutting through the heart of the old buffalo country, coming down through the shortgrass prairie, heading for the huge concrete shell embedded on the western bank of the University of Nebraska campus.

Ranchers from Kimball and Chappell. Stockbrokers from Papillion and Millard. Teachers from Columbus and Clatonia. Farmers from Gothenburg and Indianola. Realtors from Chadron and Alliance. Fans from Bancroft, Valentine, Fairbury, Red Cloud, Anselmo, Bellwood, Broken Bow, Norfolk, Oshkosh, Verdigre, Cozad, Cody, Bassett and Burwell. Families who are three-generation, season-ticket holders. Couples who plan all year for six weekends. Retirees who are taking the grandkids.

They will all come to Memorial Stadium, like they always have, filling every seat for every home game in every autumn for more than a generation.

In fact, the last time a Nebraska football team played to a less-than-sold-out Memorial Stadium, a gallon of gas cost 30 cents and a new home $12,000. Color television was just coming into view and Johnny Carson had a new job: Hosting the *Tonight Show*. *Rawhide*, *Dr. Kildare* and *Ben Casey* were trying to topple *Bonanza* as America's most popular program while Chubby Checker's *The Twist*, *Big Girls Don't Cry*, *The Monster Mash* and *Roses are Red* dominated pop music. In Liverpool, an obscure quartet released their first hit: *Love Me Do*. Tommie Frazier and Ahman Green hadn't been born and no one had ever heard of David Letterman, Oprah Winfrey, Bruce

Springsteen, the Internet, high-impact aerobics, Tombstone Pizza or Newt Gingrich. That year, President Kennedy had his hands full with Russian missiles in Cuba and riots erupted at the University of Mississippi when James Meredith tried to enroll at the all-white school. A 20-year-old Cassius Clay took out an aging Archie Moore, Wilt Chamberlain scored 100 points in a game against the Knicks and the University of Nebraska football team had recently hired a young grad assistant named Osborne.

It was October 1962.

Since then, Nebraska fans have filled Memorial Stadium for every home game for the last 33 years. That's 208 consecutive home sellouts — an ongoing NCAA record of epic proportions (Michigan, currently in second-place with 129 consecutive sellouts, trails by a staggering 13 years). Total attendance for those 208 consecutive home sellouts amounts to 15,005,249. Or put another way, if 15 million people stood finger tip-to-finger tip, the line would stretch more than 17,000 miles — roughly from Memorial Stadium to Tokyo *and back*. The aggregate home attendance is 10 times the population of Nebraska. It's approximately the population of Australia. It's the equivalent of every man, woman and child — if you will — in Denmark, Finland and Norway attending a home football game. It's equal to the City of Omaha entering and exiting Memorial Stadium 43 times; Ogallala 2,661 times; O'Neill 3,706 times; Ord 5,645 times. To equal the 15 million who have sat through the last 208 Nebraska home games, the community of Ong would have to go in and out of Memorial Stadium 144,281 times.

No matter how it's sliced, that's a lot of people.

And those are the lucky few. The chosen ones. The people who had tickets, got a seat and saw the game. What of the others? The legions of rabid fans who had neither luck, connections or geography on their side. Who couldn't rake the yard, concentrate on their son's soccer game or attend a daughter's recital because they knew it was 1 p.m. in Lincoln — on a fall Saturday. How do they cope?

Tom Mitchell, a Lincoln native long transplanted in California, offers a partial answer:

In Sacramento, there is a store on the edge of town. On a select number of Saturdays, the parking lot is often full — not with Californians picking up their weekly supply of bean sprouts, organic waffles and white wine, but with Nebraska fans tuned into the game. Seems that the store sits on a hill offering the capital city's best radio reception. And thus it is here where Big Red-starved Californians congregate, sitting in their cars, screaming and hollering, honking horns and whooping it up, occasionally confounding wary shoppers unaware of the fever from Lincoln.

Dottie Renner knows all about the fever.

She lives 650 miles east of Memorial Stadium — in Carmel, Indiana. And on fall Saturdays,

there's really no point in trying to call. The line's busy. That's because her 83-year-old mother, Hilda, who lives in Lincoln, tunes in the game, calls her daughter, and sets the receiver in front of the radio. Then her daughter and son-in-law, both Nebraska graduates, can listen to the game — all of it. The mother frequently has to listen in another room. Why? Because her daughter wants the radio turned up full blast so she can pump the play-by-play through a speaker phone. Since her

husband retired from AT&T, the Renners get a special long distance rate. So the game only costs them about $25. Still, that's cheaper than what the Renners used to do. They used to get in their car and drive to Kentucky, where they could either pick up a radio station broadcasting the game, or find a TV showing it.

And soon enough, those feverish fans without an AT&T retirement discount will have an

option, too. A new long distance telephone program recently came into being. Appropriately enough, it's called *The Husker Network*. The program is designed to do two things: Offer subscribers cheaper long distance rates and bolster the University of Nebraska-Lincoln scholarship fund. How? A percentage of revenues generated by the service will be funneled into the scholarship fund, say the owners, who have hired former Husker stars Johnny Rodgers, Jerry Tagge, Rich Glover and Mike Rozier to help market their new venture. The program is aimed at a specific market niche. In this case: Husker Fans. Collectively, they are not exactly a candidate for the endangered species list.

Nor is the consecutive home sellout streak.

As certain as the winter wind chill hitting minus double digits in Valentine, as certain as Sandhill cranes flocking in the spring to Gibbon and Kearney, as certain as farmers statewide grumbling about the horrendous summer, a stadiumful of fans will journey to Lincoln each autumn, rooting for their national championship team, extending the consecutive sellout streak well beyond all rational boundaries.

Years hence, a team of renowned sociologists may well ponder two eternal questions:

Who are these people?

And why do they keep coming...and coming...and coming?

As for the latter, the answers are diverse — some obvious, some complicated.

In part, they keep coming out of tradition and perseverance, enduring characteristics of the state. They come during warm Septembers, chilly Octobers and occasionally numbing Novembers. Elsewhere, a game-time forecast of two below, snow and gusty northwest winds might be a sure bet to empty stadiums and fill bars. At Nebraska, it merely means another sellout, with hundreds more milling outside, looking for a ticket. Descendants of people who didn't blanche at breaking sod on a frozen prairie, Memorial Stadium fans are oblivious to howling winds, harsh conditions and hardship. Two below? Snow? Gusty winds? Fine, strap on ear muffs and break out the long johns. See ya at *Barry's* afterwards.

They come, also, for another reason: Out of a collective, single-minded obsession.

A conversation overheard between two life-long Nebraska residents helps illustrate the point. A nonchalant conversation in late October:

"I can't believe the year is almost over," said the first.

"Yeah, I know," said the second. "Monday is the First of November."

"You know there are only three games left — four if you count the bowl."

"Jeez, where did this year go?"

It's true. Although there are 48 contiguous states scattered across four time zones pegged to a 52-week year, Nebraska is different. It's the only state with one time and a three-month calendar: Kickoff — September through November. There are no mountains. No Colorado Rockies to ski in, no rugged Big Sur coastline to cruise along, no Pacific Northwest rain forests to hike through. No beaches, surfing and hang-gliding. No pro teams and rival state schools to dilute loyalty, passion and focus. Nebraskans are a diverse lot and they may well debate many things: Clinton vs. Dole, Roe vs. Wade, Nature vs. Nurture, Annuities vs. IRAs. But there is little debate over the preeminent shadow cast by football across the state. It reaches a crescendo 12 weeks a year and is endlessly discussed throughout the other 40. It is the state's one big event, showcased in a flurry of red balloons, Bloody Marys, bandannas, binoculars and ballgames six or seven Saturdays a year. It is the one unifying element from Falls City to Harrison, South Sioux City to Imperial.

They come, too, for another reason — a reason unique to the state, a reason which helps illuminate the phenomenon of Nebraska football.

The Big 12 conference includes seven states with a combined population of about 36 million. Texas, population 17 million, accounts for almost half. Nebraska, with 1.6 million people, is at the other extreme. It is by far the least populated.

Kansas has a million more people. Iowa, Oklahoma and Colorado about twice as many. Missouri three times as many. Throw in all the suburbs and the cities of Dallas, Houston, Denver and St. Louis each have more people than the state of Nebraska. Yet year after year, the Nebraska varsity football roster is cluttered with Makovickas, Zatechkas, Wiegerts, Connealys, Noonans, Bennings, Bauls, Greens, Ordunas, Murtaughs, Rodgerses, Rimingtons, Schusters, Steinkuhlers and Tony Davises. Kids from Tecumseh, Ord, Burr, Cozad, Fremont, Brainard, Fullerton, Battle Creek, St. Paul, Hartington, Waverly, Grand Island, Lincoln and Omaha.

There is no other Division 1 football program — ever — which derives more from a sparse, home-grown talent base than Nebraska, a state ranking 15th in size, but 36th in population. Simply stated, from the Nemaha to the Niobrara — less is more.

A glance at the 1996 team roster underscored the point:

Of the 11 projected offensive starters, nine are Nebraska kids.

Three of the five offensive lineman are from Lincoln.

Two others — the split end and a guard — are from Cozad.

The tight end is from Columbus.

The first three I-backs are from Omaha.

The first three fullbacks are from Fullerton, Brainard and Elgin.

The first three quarterbacks are from Wood River, Wahoo and Kearney.

While other Division 1 powers routinely mine the talent-rich gold fields of Los Angeles, Miami, Dallas, Houston, Pittsburgh and Detroit, Nebraska is harvesting recruits and attracting walk-ons from places a Penn State recruiter can't pronounce, has never heard of — and probably couldn't find with a map. To wit: The enrollment at Dallas Carter High School is greater than the combined population of the three towns that Nebraska's fullbacks call home.

And there is a strong link between those homes and the home of the Huskers.

Put another way: When a kid from tiny Osceola journeys to Lincoln, perseveres and eventually makes the team, he creates a built-in fan club stretching from the local swimming pool to the Dairy Queen. People who coached his Peewee team, cleaned up his grammar, cut his hair, caught him flinging snowballs, told him where the best fishing holes were and rooted for him at state tournament time. Multiply it out by hundreds of kids from scores of communities over four decades and there is a kind of populist, grass-roots, bedrock fandom encompassing every gully and grain tower from Homestead National Monument to Chimney Rock. A tightly woven, cultural fabric wholly unique to a place the Otoe Indians once called "flat water."

No one, perhaps, understands this link better than the coach. Born and raised in Hastings, a graduate of Hastings High School, a graduate of Hastings College, holder of a Ph.D. in educational psychology from the University of Nebraska, Tom Osborne arrived the year the sellout streak began and has never left. Scour Division 1 waters and how many native sons are still afloat? Have been there for 33 years? Have kept the coaching staff relatively in tact across three decades? Have won consecutive national championships? Have produced the most GTE Academic All-Americans among Division 1 schools?

Only one.

But, in truth, Nebraska Fans journey to Memorial Stadium for the most primitive, fundamental reason of all: Build a better team — and they will come.

At Nebraska, the better football team wins...and wins...and wins. And then it wins some more.

And so their fans keep coming.

Heading into the 1996 season, Nebraska fans were following a football team that boasted the nation's longest winning streak (25 games) and the longest home winning streak (30 games). In one three-year stretch, several Huskers had never played in a losing regular season game. In those years — 1993-1995 — Nebraska accomplished what no other Division 1 football team ever has: Won 36 games in a three-year period. Mid-way

through the decade, the team had won five consecutive conference championships, posted four consecutive undefeated home stands, completed three consecutive undefeated regular seasons, garnered two national championships and compiled a 38-2 record at Memorial Stadium.

In fact, every Nebraska football player who has journeyed to Lincoln since 1969 and completed four years, has left with at least one

Big Eight championship ring and gone to four bowl games.

Not coincidentally, many of the streaks unique to Nebraska began about the same time a jovial Irishman from Michigan landed in Lincoln. The impact Bob Devaney had on Nebraska football was both immediate and enduring. In 1961, under Coach Bill Jennings, the Huskers went 3-6-1. In 1962, under first-year Coach Devaney, the team

went 9-2. In Devaney's first five years, the team compiled a 47-8-0 record and neither Nebraska nor its football has been the same since. In 1969, Nebraska won its last seven games, again finishing 9-2. That began yet another pair of streaks: 27 consecutive nine-win seasons (an NCAA record) and 27 consecutive bowl appearances, including 15 straight New Year's games. In 1970 and 1971, Devaney led Nebraska to consecutive national championships and the legend became firmly entrenched.

Many years later, Devaney was asked to identify his most lasting memory of life in Lincoln. His answer: The fans.

"I was very pleased with their interest and enthusiasm — the way they filled up that stadium right from the beginning. They are the best fans in the country....I think that's probably the thing I'll remember most — more than any single event."

Upon arriving from the University of Wyoming, Bob Devaney had but one serious complaint: He had left behind better facilities in Laramie.

It was true. Back then, Memorial Stadium was a Studebaker of a stadium, a crude, simple, industrial-strength, standard-issue job: Two slabs of concrete stands — one east, one west. Open on the north and south, save for a few wooden bleachers. A capacity of 31,000. The press box was late Roman era; the visitors' quarters early Appalachia. The cheesiest carnival barker had a better sound system. In 1962, a ticket for an adult cost four bucks. Kids had two choices: Fork over 50 cents and sit in the Knot Hole Section, or simply sneak in. Either way, it didn't seem to matter much.

Flash forward and the Stubebaker has evolved into a Mercedes. Painted, polished and spit-shined. A massive bowl seating 76,000. Plush green carpeting. Towering, state-of-the art HuskerVision screens, instant replays in living color. Thumping Tunnel Music pumped through hi-tech sound systems. A spacious field house for visitors, a sprawling, modern press box for scribes. Ex-Knot Holers cashing in their four bits for a seat in the posh, glass-encased VIP section. A single-game ticket now costs $28 and the Knot Hole Section has long gone the way of the Studebaker.

Although the stadium, players, coaches and fans may have changed along the way, one constant remains: winning. What Devaney started, Tom Osborne continued.

Numbers help tell the story.

In the 33 years since the home sellout streak began, Nebraska has:

Sold out 208 consecutive home games.

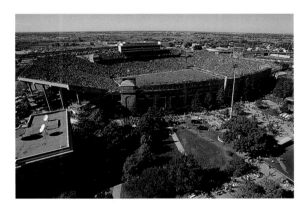

Compiled a home record of 183 wins and 25 losses, a winning rate of 88 percent.

Posted 34 consecutive winning seasons.

Completed 16 unbeaten and untied home seasons.

Appeared in 31 bowl games, including an NCAA record 27 in a row.

Finished in the final Top 20 rankings 26 consecutive years, an on-going NCAA record.

Won 4 National Championships.

Claimed 19 conference championships.

Taken 12 NCAA rushing titles, including four of the last five.

Along the way, the team has produced:

Two Heisman Trophy winners.

Seven Outland Trophy winners.

Three Lombardi Award winners.

One Butkus Award winner.

Fifty-five All-Americans.

Forty-nine Academic All-Americans.

It has long been a cliché that, on six or seven Saturdays a year, Nebraska football fans turn Memorial Stadium into the state's third-largest city, a city that contains one-twentieth of the state's population, a city of 76,000 residents. From atop Oldfather Hall, they appear as an indistinguishable mass, a fuzzy, unfocused blur, a kind of Matisse or Renoir heavy on the red.

At street level, the focus sharpens, and the residents of Memorial Stadium begin to look like those of any other city. They have faces and clearly defined features. They are families and married couples. Senior citizens and middle-aged men and women. Young children and college students. Infants and teenagers. Tall, thin, short, squat. Black, white, red and brown. And like any city, they have chores to tend to, certain jobs to do, specific tasks to perform. Individuals working for the collective good.

On the pages inside are photographs and stories of some of these individuals, the residents of Memorial Stadium, the fans who — on a half-dozen Saturdays each autumn — constitute one of America's most interesting communities.

For instance:

Resting comfortably inside a 37-foot Coachmen about an hour before kickoff, there is an elderly wiener dog who went to every home and away game in 1995, including the Fiesta Bowl. If his owners return in high spirits, he, too, is euphoric, jumping around, licking and kissing, maniacally wagging his 14-year-old tail. If they don't, he gets depressed and slinks off to a corner,

pouting, unapproachable, incommunicative. For a long time now, Basil's depressions have been few and far between.

Somewhere outside the stadium, probably on the highway, there is the proud driver of a white 1996 Peterbilt Model 377 18-wheeler semi. In 1995, his employers, the Seward Motor Freight Company, selected Mitch Krolikowski as their driver of the year. His reward: He got to fill his

53-foot trailer with tons of Nebraska weight-training equipment and truck them to Tempe for the Fiesta Bowl. He also got two game tickets, Husker caps, T-shirts and an autographed football. "It was a great honor to do it. And I'll tell you what -- I was all worked up for that game," said the Loup City resident. The trek to Tempe went fine, except for a few rough spots in Oklahoma. Seems some of the Okie truckers

took exception to a semi angling through Sooner Country with a lot of Husker decals on it. "One guy got on his CB and asked me what all those nasty stickers were all about. I explained it to him and he ended up thinking it was pretty cool."

Heading toward the stadium there is a couple whose holiday home becomes a blazing image of mixed metaphors late each year. On the lawn outside of Craig and Tina Staehr's house, the traditional Santa and reindeer appear in the foreground. Behind them, in the back-ground, there is the traditional nativity scene — Joseph, Mary and the baby Jesus. Were wise men to follow the shining star overhead, however, it would deliver them unto a different kind of holy land. One in which Herbie Husker appears beneath a white-hot, mega-wattage sign proclaiming: "Nebraska National Champs 1994-95." A star that blazes brightly night after night above "Big 8 Champs," "Go Big Red" and a Nebraska helmet with the trademark "N." A star that burns above a house that, just for good measure, sports the opponent and score of each game — all trimmed in hundreds of flashing, red-and-white lights.

Deep in the bowels of the North Field House, there is a 63-year-old man who still walks to the stadium from his boyhood home, arriving most mornings well before dawn. In 1962, the year the sellout streak began, he became the head grounds keeper. For 33 years, he has shoveled snow from the field, chipped ice off the seats, sprinkled sawdust in waterholes, opened the gates, ushered in the concessionaires and supervised the four-day cleanup after every home game. "When I first got here, I was as big as most of the players," said the burly ex-Marine. "Now you couldn't find me in the huddle with a pair of binoculars."

Outside, up in the east stadium, the Reverend has just arrived. He started attending games the year World War II ended, riding the rails from Axtell to Lincoln and back. Now he arrives in a flaming, candy-apple red pickup truck. Back home in Cook, the Lutheran minister has but one firm rule for his congregation: "I tell them right up front — 'Don't even think about scheduling any weddings or funerals on game days.'"

Far below, down on the track, the Dawson County Public Defender already has his game face on. And his red-and-white striped shirt.

And red slacks rolled up to white knees, above red socks and red Nikes. A long pony tail spills out from beneath his red-and-white ball cap. The public defender was up about 6 a.m. Checking the weather report. He wanted to know if there'd be a tail wind or a head wind come kickoff. It could affect his one surpassing skill: Firing a hot dog in a tight spiral 25 rows deep with precision accuracy.

Years ago, he rode a motorcycle, had long hair and eschewed a suit and tie. And he was also up for the job of Hall County Attorney. The commissioners laid it on the line: The job was his — under four conditions. "I did a lot of soul searching that weekend and I could kind of understand not riding the motorcycle anymore. I could kind of understand getting a haircut. And I could kind of understand maybe getting a suit and tie. But give up throwing the 'dogs? Never!"

High atop the West Stadium — in Section D, Row 2 — of the glass-enclosed press box, there is the reigning patriarch of Nebraska Football Fans. His personal home-game streak makes the 208 consecutive sellouts seem like a lost footnote, a trivial afterthought. Between the time he saw his first game and the fall of 1995, many Husker fans were born, graduated from high school, married, had raised a family, played with their grandchildren — and then died of old age. The man in Section D has been to every Nebraska home game for the last 70 years.

Just down the aisle, not far away, there is...well — there really is no place like Nebraska.

● *The Night Before*

Not all of the 76,000 Memorial Stadium fans visit *Misty's* on the night before a home game — it just seems that way.

Walk in around 7 p.m. Friday and you can be sure of one thing: There will be more people eating more food, quaffing more refreshments, immersed in more revelry, amid more noise and general chaos than in any restaurant since those heady days immediately preceding the collapse of The Roman Empire.

There is, to be sure, a method to the madness and it doesn't take a Columbo, a Mickey Spillane or Sherlock Holmes to figure out what that might be. The expansive lobby offers a subtle clue: Upon row after row of glass-encased shelves lie row after row of Nebraska football helmets, NFL helmets worn by ex-Nebraska football players, autographed Nebraska footballs, autographed photos of Nebraska players and the general sort of assorted bric-a-brac that only a serious fan could possess. In effect, the lobby is a kind of museum dedicated to the proposition that not all football teams are necessarily created equal. That the one in Lincoln may be something special.

And that's just the lobby. Inside, of course, there is, well...

There is KLIN's Jim Rose, parked in one packed corner with a mobile station unit,

engulfed by fans, adding a little fuel to the Big Red fire with a live broadcast that will be picked up by more than 200 stations statewide.

There is Coach George Darlington, architect of the defensive secondary, hemmed in by a mob of well wishers, fielding congratulations, fielding questions, fielding a significantly greater wall of blockers than his troops will encounter the next day.

Not far away is a football-shaped bar stacked seven and eight rows deep with a high-octane mass of Husker faithful high-fiving old friends and new acquaintances beneath a canopy of streamers, confetti and balloons that occasionally drift across the way to a dining room over-whelmed with clusters of families and friends and fans whose tables peek out from beneath huge platters of potatoes, prime rib and porter-house, beneath stacks of bread and bottles of beer, beneath salads, French fries, apple pie and ice cream.

At a point when it seems impossible to ratchet the fever another notch — at about 9 p.m. — a door bursts open on the second floor and out explodes the University of Nebraska Pep Band and the varsity cheerleaders and Herbie Husker and then they all commence to march down the swarming aisles, pompons whirling, bold brass instruments ablaze with a deafening rendition of the Husker fight song. Before the last note ends, a thunderous chant begins to buckle the ear drums, sweeping through the lobby, around the KLIN corner, across the bar, past Darlington, over the dining room and beyond: **"GO BIG RED! GO BIG RED! GO BIG RED!"** Herbie is in his ele-ment now and is making the rounds, patting the heads of small children, shaking the hands of large adults, finally emerging in a back party room strewn with red-and-white balloons and about 50 of the hard core. When he appears in the doorway, they begin to chant his name and then the pep band shows up and soon there is an impromptu dance in the middle of the room and that would be Herbie doing the jig with an elderly woman — until a middle-aged man shows up, steps between them and says, with utter can-dor: "Herbie, I love you, man."

More than 30 years ago, **Bob Milton** opened *Misty's Restaurant & Lounge* in a tiny, nondescript building off Havelock Avenue in northeast Lincoln. Gutted by fire in 1976, it was exten-sively remodeled and has been a fan favorite ever since.

It seats 600 now and Milton says he turns the tables two-and-a-half times on a typical, pre-game Friday night, serving about 1,500 for dinner, or approximately the community of Fullerton. But, then, he's not unnerved by crowds.

"For a while, I used to throw an annual pig party for the team at my house," said Milton. "For all the football players, all the basketball players, all the coaches, their wives and their friends. One year, about 600 people showed up. We had a ball."

He also used to hire some of the players to work the door, tend bar, sign autographs, even do a little cooking back in the kitchen. "Jerry Tagge, Jerry Murtaugh and Wally Winter — they were some of my all-time favorites."

Maybe it was something in the water that year. 1962. The year *Misty's* opened. The year Devaney arrived in Lincoln. The year Osborne joined the team. The year the sellout streak began. The year the university appointed a new head grounds keeper.

His name is **Bill Shepard** and he's instantly recognizable by the red cap with white polka dots he has worn for so long now that perhaps it can only be removed through surgery.

By 6 a.m. on game days he's been in his "office" beneath the North Field House for a good half hour, maybe longer. With 76,000 visitors coming, there is plenty to do. Shortly after 6, he and his crew of three full-time assistants swing open the massive stadium gates, ushering in the first wave of concessionaires. Then the astro-turf field must be swept. Then around 7 a.m. all the electricians and plumbers arrive. Then all the ticket cans have to be put out. And the sideline markers set up. And the goal post pads attached. Hopefully, the weather will be decent. No snow to shovel. Ice to chip off. Salt and sand to spread around. After the game, it's lock down and everything is reversed. Everything has to be taken down and put back in. Then on Sunday, at 5:30 a.m., Shepard and his crew arrive to orchestrate the serious clean-up. ROTC members pick up all the papers, boxes, cartons and wrappers and sweep the stadium aisles. On Monday, the blowers come out, propelling cigarette butts and peanut shells from the stands. By nightfall Wednesday, in a perfect world, Memorial Stadium will appear as though no one had visited four days earlier.

It's a lot of work and Shepard loves it, feeling sorry, in fact, for those who've sold their soul for money, are bored and frustrated in passionless avocations.

"There just aren't many who get to do what they really love and when I start to worry about getting up and getting over here, that's when I'm done. But it hasn't happened yet."

At 63, six-feet and 190 pounds, he looks 20 years younger — and it appears he could keep fussing over the stadium's appearance for at least that long. He awakes at 4:20 each morning, arriving at the stadium by 5:30. Often, he walks the two miles from his home — the same home the Lincoln native grew up in. After a stint in the Marines, he began working for the university in 1948. He became an assistant grounds keeper in 1960 and got the head job two years later. For 33 years, he has been able to adapt to a multitude of changes — all but the weather. It can still produce a sleepless Friday night.

"I remember one K-State game where it had snowed like crazy and we got out on the field at halftime to get rid of it. Well, the K-State coaches were furious. They wanted the snow to stay because it was kind of an equalizer. It took an extra 30 minutes, but we finally got it all off. And, of course, we ended up winning the game, too."

Among his many memories, he said, are the great Nebraska fans and a number of players. "Johnny Rodgers was one of the really great kids we had here. It was always 'Mr. This' and 'Mr. That' and 'thank you' all the time. And Richie Glover. Now that was a really great kid, too.

"Everything around here — including me — has changed so much. Everything but the fundamentals. You still have to hit, catch and throw."

There's one other thing that hasn't changed, said Shepard.

"I've been all over the world and believe me, it's true what they say. There's no place like home."

A mid-October breeze sweeps in from the north. So chilly this morning that gloves, jackets and hooded sweatshirts are *de rigueur*. What better time then to set up a card table in an exposed, empty parking lot and have a picnic? Not a picnic really, but a tail-gate party. Not a tail-gate party, actually, but a hood party. That's the thinking that has led **Don** and **Norma Goure**, **Cecil Martin** and **Norm Smith** to Parking Lot No. 9 on the northeast side of Memorial Stadium. Kickoff is only four hours and seven minutes away and the hood of their car is still warm from the drive down from Bellevue, so they are bundled in red jackets, red sweatshirts, red hats, red socks and red shoes, huddled around a table sprouting peanuts, Pringles and tomato juice next to the toasty hood of their car in the middle of the aforementioned cold, windy, empty parking lot.

"We love Nebraska football," allows Norma, in what a college writing instructor might identify as an example of "understatement." "We love the camaraderie. When we bring guests down here from out-of-state, they are always amazed at the sight, the scene, the crowd, all the red, the following that Nebraska football has."

Norm has been a part of that following since 1950, when he regularly used to drive in from Ogallala, 550 miles roundtrip. "We went to the Orange Bowl last year and we talked to a Miami guy and he said he couldn't begin to understand Nebraska fans. He said Miami fans would go to the Orange Bowl to see their team, but that's about it. He saw the thousands of us in the stands and he just shook his head. I guess it's kind of hard to explain to outsiders. They don't really understand."

The parking lot faithful understand one another perfectly. It is an alliance forged on asphalt lots, concrete highways, at campground hook-ups and mostly, of course, as fast-flowing tributaries feeding that ceaseless sea of red. Within the Kingdom of Husker Fans, these are the people who constitute a species unto themselves. The Parking Lot RV Fan. A community of people who think nothing of unhitching their 25-foot Winnebagos and galloping off on a week-long, 2,000-mile journey to see a three-hour game. They are, perhaps, the hardest of the hard core. They keep tabs on one another, inspect each others' RVs, trade oil-change and road-wear secrets, swap campground information, exchange short-cut and back-road tips, barter beer for steak and are adept at circling their hi-tech Conestogas in enemy territory from Miami to Boulder, East Lansing to Stillwater.

But they love home games the most.

Ask **Tom Hilt** and **Bob Cole**. They've just landed at Lot No. 9 in something that would be called a C-130 Hercules if it had wings, something Schwarzkopf probably could have used in Desert Storm. It's actually an RV — roughly the length of Lake McConaughy, an RV in which some passengers, those in the back, are probably in the Mountain Time Zone. Technically, it's called a "Prevo" and it's the game-day vehicle of choice for a large group of Omaha-area fans. For home games, the routine never varies. They meet early Saturday at one of the their homes. Have coffee, rolls and orange juice. Toss the football around a bit. Then leave at precisely 10 a.m. — once stranding 15 people who arrived late. Arriving at the stadium lot between 11 and 11:30, they have either a box lunch, or barbecue on some of the 2,000 to 3,000 portable grills which emerge from beneath the Prevo's side panels. After the game, they repair to the Prevo's salon for soup and sandwiches and warm drinks, catching up on other college games on the Prevo's color TV, waiting for traffic to clear out. They're back home by 6:30. Been doing it for 10 years.

Many are members of the Husker Power Club, including Tom, who is on the board of directors. The group sponsored a recent raffle that netted $13,000 for the athletic department.

"We love the tradition and integrity of Nebraska football," said Bob. "We all like being a part of the state's third-largest city. We think we're the best fans in the world."

A sentiment apparently not shared by at least one Kansas resident.

It happened when the Prevo was enroute to Manhattan for a road game at Kansas State. It's true that the Nebraska Fight Song may have been a contributing factor. It blasted from the Prevo's external speakers while deep in enemy territory that day. But still...

At a stop sign in Hiawatha a large man in a pickup truck got out, turned his broad backside to the Prevo...and dropped his drawers. Hung a full moon on them. Right on Main Street, middle of the morning. "Then he got back in his truck,"

said Tom, "and just drove away. Like it was the most normal thing in the world."

Hard to say what **Orville Olson** might have done. Back home in Cook, Nebraska, he's the Rev. Olson, a man of the cloth. Yet he knows as well as any the passions that drive good men over the brink on football Saturdays. After all, it is the Reverend himself, standing no more than 100 feet from the warm-hood party, no more than 50 feet from the Prevo, who said it first: "I guess I've got two religions to deal with. I actually tell people I take on tours of the stadium that they're standing on holy ground."

The Reverend's obsession has spread to its 50th year, its fourth generation. In the pre-war years, his parents were season ticket holders. Now, he and his wife are swathed in red and "all of our children wear red and they dress all of our grandchildren in red — from head to toe — every game day. In our family, there's a lot of pride in being a good fan."

No one inside the 27-foot Winnebago idling down the way from Olson's red pickup would disagree with the Reverend's latest sermon. It's warming up now, kickoff less than three hours, when the door opens and out pop two diminutive blondes clutching red-and-white pompons, each sporting a red "N" and "#1" on her forehead. Only 10:30 and 12-year-old **Sarah Wees** and her 9-year-old sister, **Lisa**, have already been to "The Big Red Shop" for decals, stickers, pennants and tattoos, to *Barry's* for 7-Up and back to the Winnebago for a pre-game lunch.

Their grandparents, **Frank** and **Jeanette Semin**, of Bellevue, are among the RV road warriors now beginning to overwhelm the vast parking lot. "We took the girls on a road trip to Missouri last year," says Jeanette, "and that's where they started their cheerleading: 'Nebraska Rules — Missouri Drools.'" Frank, meanwhile, tries to affect a studied nonchalance. "I only come to these things because my wife loves football," is how it's stated. Jeanette, naturally, is more than willing to set the record straight. Seems that Frank actually started coming in the late 50s, when he and some of his fraternity brothers at Creighton University would reserve two cars and train down to Lincoln.

Now he drives the Winnebago, its two flags snapping proudly in the October breeze. "We always like to fly the American flag with our Nebraska flag," says Jeanette.

Behind the Winnebago is a 37-foot Coachmen. An observer carefully trained to decipher meaning from the smallest detail can tell by the "Cornhuskers On Board" sign and the 17 different Nebraska football helmets, the 71 different Herbies and the 46 different red-and-white cheerleader dolls in the front window that the driver of this particular vehicle did not make a wrong turn and accidentally end up in Lot 9 of Memorial Stadium on a fall Saturday approximately 127 minutes before kickoff.

When it comes to Nebraska football, it is clear within minutes that the RV's occupants — **Harold** and **Ann Tell** and **Charlie** and **Betty Soderberg** — know exactly what they're doing. Former classmates at Wakefield High School, they now journey to home and away games with a precision that would shame a Green Beret unit. For home games, it goes something like this: The Tells, who retired to Branson, Missouri, in 1989, drive their RV to the Greenwood Campground, where they meet up with the Sodenbergs,

who drive their RV from Wakefield, on Friday afternoon. They spend the evening at the campground and then on Saturday morning, one RV stays behind and they all pile into the other and head for the stadium. After arriving, Harold assumes command of the kitchen, creating a breakfast of pancakes, scrambled eggs, bacon, orange juice and coffee. About 90 minutes before kickoff large Bloody Marys appear. When they hear the marching band, the door opens and they head for their seats. Afterwards, there is dinner at the American Legion Club, then back to the campground. Sunday morning, there is a farewell breakfast and a final tactical session to confirm logistics for the next game.

Basil, the Tells' 14-year-old dachshund, is as committed to the Husker cause as any of the group's bipeds. On this fine fall day, he appears somewhat dashing. Sporting a natty red-and-white scarf, the elderly bon vivant is ensconced in a rear lounge seat, taking in a little sun before the game. "If we win the game," says Harold, "we always come back and say 'Go Big Red' and then he'll start barking and wagging his tail and jumping around like crazy."

☉ Noon

The autumn sun is arcing overhead and the breeze kicks up again, hurtling gold and amber leaves through the streets, across campus, down the sidewalks, past the Lee and Helene Sapp Recreation Center and the Student Union. The people, too, are in a hurry. There is a sense of urgency now. Diverse and far-flung pre-game rituals suddenly give way to a unified focus as tens of thousands of feet begin an accelerated march toward the stadium gates. Herbie has abandoned his post in front of the Nebraska Bookstore and is closing in on Love Memorial Library. A pedestrian skyway on North Tenth Street, empty a few hours earlier, is seriously full. From the south, fans pour through campus, moving briskly past the Sheldon Memorial Art Gallery, scuttling along sidewalks, between the hedges, toward their seats. From the east and west come thousands more and soon a swirling mass of red temporarily transforms the stadium perimeter into a kind of open-air, gridiron bazaar.

Uncle Sam has two tickets he's trying to unload. Around the bend, another fan — who, for reasons unknown, is trying to bike through the mob — happens to need two tickets. In between, a young Hulk Hogan wannabee flashes his bulk

not far from an elderly fan wearing a sweater embossed with a hand-made red "N." Behind her, a father and son leisurely enjoy a slice of pizza or two, across the way from 7-year-old **Benny Holmes**. A nascent Nebraska fan-turned-entrepreneur, he's working the crowd pretty well, hawking souvenir papers at a crowded campus intersection. And he's not alone. The balloon girls are out in force, too. That would be **Kara Thompson**, of Sioux Falls, South Dakota, and **Emily Point**, from Rochester, Minnesota, both 20, both UNL juniors, both Pi Beta Phi Sorority sisters, both clutching a fistful of red balloons, both working their first home game. Veteran Officer **Milo Bushing**, meanwhile, resplendent in his UNL police uniform, calmly surveys the sight, the sound, the scene, all the people who are beginning to move quickly toward the gates on the east side of Memorial Stadium.

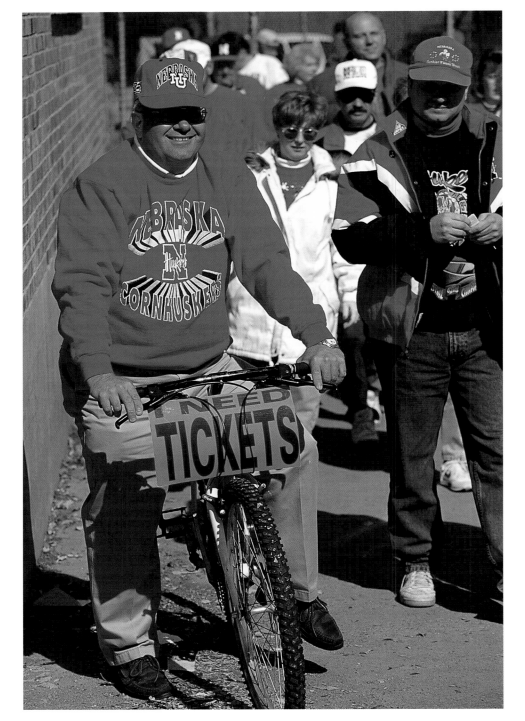

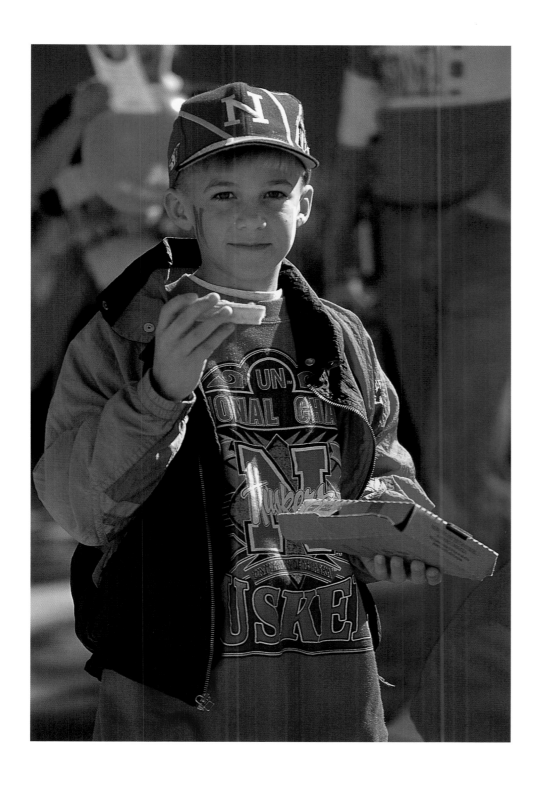

There are perhaps several hundred Memorial Stadium fans, maybe more, who know something the other 75,000-plus do not. They know the reason Nebraska wins so many home games. They know it's not because of Bob Devaney or Tom Osborne or Jeff Kinney or Turner Gill or Tommie Frazier. It's because of **Les Roberts**.

Les Roberts is not a former I-back, a coach, a career scout or an X and O wizard. He's a ticket taker. He's worked the same gate — Gate 20, East Stadium — for the last 32 years, missing two home games during that span. "One was when I was singing in 'The Lincoln Continentals,' which is a Barbershop Quartet, and we had to go to Wichita for a contest. The only other time was when my son was playing in a reserve football game for Southeast that was at Grand Island and I couldn't get back in time."

And you'd a thought he'd joined the Communist Party. Or a devil-worshiping cult. Or moved to Oklahoma. His people weren't happy — and they let him know it. Understand this: His people are chronically superstitious, perhaps pathologically so. They come to the same gate, his gate, game after game, and expect him, Les Roberts, to take their ticket, year after year.

And he does.

"They won't go in any other gate," says Les. "They've told me they don't want to jinx the team. They're afraid if they go through another gate and someone else takes their ticket that the team will lose. A bunch of them have said they don't know what they're going to do when I'm not around anymore."

Here's the good news: At 62, Les Roberts has never been sick on game day. And he has no plans for early retirement.

When he arrived at his ticket-taking station more than three decades ago, he did so with a good deal of Big Red momentum. A Tecumseh native, Roberts graduated from NU in 1958 and later taught at the university. A football ticket has been his link to the stadium for almost half-a-century. "My father got the ticket first and then he passed it down to me. I gave it to my wife and now she won't give it up. She comes through my gate and sits in exactly the same seat my father did in the late 40s."

Maybe it's just as well that his wife has the one ticket he can't take. Through the years, he's made countless friends from across the state and said he can probably greet 200 or so by their first name.

One thing to remember, however: You do need a ticket to pass through Gate 20 - East Stadium. At Nebraska home games, desperation is the mother of invention. And Les has seen his share of inventive desperadoes. Like the fella who rushed up wearing an apron and a cardboard box on his head. Said he was with concessions. Had to get right in and start selling. "It was a nice try, probably one of the better ones. But it didn't work."

The bazaar is winding down and the big show is not far away and so they are storming Gate 20 and all the other gates now from all directions. On the east, a large group masses below the huge red "N" on the stadium wall. Then a father and son arrive in tandem, thrusting their tickets forward, and soon they and their identical shaved heads — painted in the form of Nebraska football helmets — pass through a south gate. An elderly group is perched along one edge of the West Stadium, waiting for a second wind, getting ready for a final assault of the steps. Overhead, an outside ramp appears in muted silhouette, hundreds of shadowy figures shuffling upward, closer and closer to their final destination.

No matter how many times it happens, the scene remains unforgettable. Climb the last step, walk the last foot, pass through the doorway and there it is: One-twentieth of Nebraska's population laid out in neat rows of red beneath an open sky, above an endless prairie. There isn't much time now, but there is plenty to occupy the remaining minutes. The nation's No. 1 university marching band struts its stuff across an electric-green playing field. The sound system booms with a power and clarity that carries through downtown streets. Cameras linked to the towering HuskerVision screens overhead scour the stands for interesting visuals, for unusual sights. There is no shortage, to be sure. Pictures help tell the story.

Five minutes and counting and it is now abundantly clear that a big-time college football program is about to unleash all of its home-game fury on a visiting team whose first-year players might be thinking that their mothers hadn't been entirely wrong about the many advantages of tennis, who might be wondering if the Christian vs. Lion match hadn't produced better odds. They have come to these unnerving conclusions based largely on a PA system that has loosened their cleats and those Vermont-sized color screens that keep showing replays of last week's game in which Nebraska's defense entered the enemy backfield in a manner reminiscent of Allied troops hitting Omaha Beach. It doesn't help that Herbie is cavorting frenetically along the home-team sidelines and that the tuba player is possibly larger than their nose guard and that maybe one or two of the cheerleaders is faster than their tailback. And, of course, right behind Herbie and the band and the cheerleaders there is a row of half-naked fans streaked in red body paint who are yelling and screaming directly in front of another young fan who looks as though

he may well be AWOL from the Henry Doorly compound. Nor could it have been comforting to the young men along the west sidelines who were trying to steel their nerves minutes before kickoff when they suddenly heard the first eerie strains of this strange music and looked up at the screens and saw there were many large bodies massed in a tunnel and soon they had all moved to a gate beneath the South Stadium and that's when their coach gave a signal and then they all came charging onto the field to a collective roar deafening enough to de-tassel corn in Seward.

Months, weeks, days, hours — they've all winnowed down to this moment and then the ball floats skyward and home-team helmets are held aloft and a crimson carpet of 76,000 rises en masse, watching 22 young men hurl their bodies at one another from a multitude of angles. Soon, there is an intensity that overwhelms, a delicate balance of raw speed and brute power orchestrated by subtle strategies and deft maneuvers. The coach is on the sidelines, clipboard in hand, fine-tuning the march in increments of 5, 10, 15 yards. Players shuttle in and out, back and forth and their teammates slide closer and closer to the edge of the bench, straining to watch the blur of bodies piling up, then unpiling, then piling up again. The chain-gang crew scrambles to keep up and the field grows shorter and shorter until the referee finally thrusts his arms overhead and then the band kicks it into high gear and the cheerleaders launch into perfect somersaults and a thunderous wall of sound crashes through Memorial Stadium. Momentarily, the sky overhead is a mosaic of red dots.

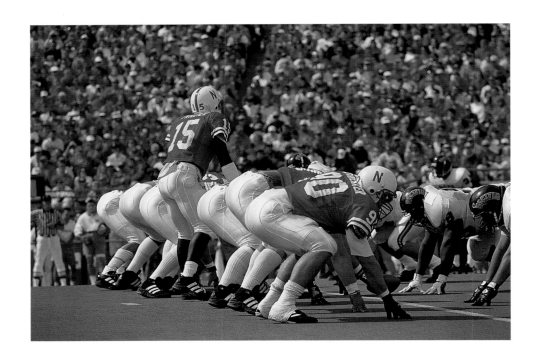

Robert L. Rowe lived for these moments. And died for them.

An obituary printed in the Sept. 9, 1991, *Lincoln Journal-Star* officially identified him as "Robert L. 'Husker Bob' Rowe." A Nebraska native, he was an army infantryman in World War II. On the South Pacific island of New Guinea, Rowe once was hemmed in while on patrol and spent nine days in a cave before comrades rescued him.

More than 30 years later, comrades again came to his rescue.

It was 1978 and it began innocently enough. A friend asked if he'd like to attend a Nebraska home football game. He said he would. But he found the South Stadium fans obnoxious, so he decided to get up, cut across the field and head for the band section. Stadium security didn't like the idea. That's when band members raced to his rescue. By the fourth game, the band had wangled permission for Rowe to sit with them...And a legend was born.

Exit Robert L. Rowe. Enter Husker Bob.

For the next 13 years, Husker Bob Super Fan turned Memorial Stadium into his own personal pulpit. No part of the stadium was too remote to deliver the message. Layered bootheel to cap in red

and white, he roamed the stadium in a frenzy, carrying signs, waving flags, unfurling pennants, leading cheers, imploring the faithful to yell a little harder, scream a little louder, get those Husker juices flowing. Conference foes weren't even safe in their own stadium. Sometimes he and friends would drive to away games. Sometimes radio announcers would load him up in their van and they'd hit the road together. A printer by trade, he knew Devaney. He knew a lot of the players. He knew most of the band members. And he knew hundreds of his fellow fans.

The first heart attack occurred on Saturday, Nov. 7, 1987, a few hours after the Nebraska-Iowa State game. He talked about slowing down a bit. But it didn't happen. Soon, he was popping up at wrestling matches. And at volleyball, basketball, baseball and softball games.

The second heart attack, a fatal one, occurred on Saturday, Sept. 7, 1991, shortly after a home game against Utah State. For Robert L. "Husker Bob" Rowe, it can literally be said: He lived and died Nebraska football.

◐ 2:15 PM

Along about halftime, the pre-game brunches have worn off and hunger is becoming an issue. Some fans will leave their seats in search of food. Others will stay put, waiting for it to find them.

P. Stephen Potter is a man of many talents. He is an accomplished attorney at law and a connoisseur of plains Indian art. He enjoys frequent trips to Central America and has climbed Devil's Tower. He is an avid scuba diver, mountain biker, downhill skier and white-water kayaker.

Of his many skills, one endures as the most gratifying: "I enjoy most what I do best — throwing hotdogs."

It's not enough that Nebraska boasts the nation's No. 1 football team, the No. 1 volleyball team, the No. 1 marching band, the NIT mens' basketball champions, gymnastics and wrestling powerhouses, world record-holders in swimming and world-class athletes in track and field. Now, among the hundreds of hotdog vendors nationwide, the one man who arguably throws the tightest spiral the greatest distance with the most accuracy over the longest period of time is P. Stephen Potter, Dawson County Public Defender,

Gothenburg native, the bearded guy with the long pony tail and short pants pitching strike after strike into the sun-washed stands of Memorial Stadium.

Like all world-class athletes, Potter did not arrive at No. 1 overnight. He has trained long and hard, beginning in 1964, the year he first started throwing hotdogs while a Nebraska Pharmacy College student. He graduated in 1969, kept throwing the 'dogs during his Law School days at Creighton and has never stopped. In 32 years, he has missed two games: one due to a hospitalized illness; the other due to his wedding. Using Potter's estimate of 400 tosses a game during six games a year for 32 years, he has thrown, interestingly enough, about 76,000 hotdogs — or roughly one 'dog for every fan in Memorial Stadium, plus a few hundred left over for coaches, players, referees, Herbie and the chain-gang crew.

At 51, however, he can no longer rely on raw physical talent. Instead, he has evolved into a wily veteran, using science and meticulous planning to elevate his game and prolong his career. On the Friday before a home game, he will leave Gothenburg, where he maintains a private practice, and drive to Lincoln, where he maintains an apartment, arriving about 8:30 p.m. Shortly after dawn Saturday, he anxiously clicks on the Weather Channel, awaiting a resolution to the critical question: Which side of the stadium will he work that day? The answer is blowing in the wind.

"It's very difficult to throw a tight spiral into the wind," Potter explains. "So what I'm hoping to hear on the weather report is that there'll be a steady wind blowing from northeast to southwest. That will allow me to work the West Stadium, where my best customers are. A steady wind from that direction becomes a tail wind, which favors a righthander, and it will produce tighter spirals and greater accuracy."

If he's lucky, the forecast also will include afternoon highs in the low 60s. "If it's too warm, people won't eat as much. If it's too chilly, they like to keep their hands in their pockets." If he gets the right wind, the right temperature *and* a blowout game — well, we're talking conditions that verge on the transcendent. "If it's a romp, they are as likely to be entertained by my throws as the game."

As is true of most people who've been at the top of their game as long as Potter, he has his own collection of "Greatest Hits," a highlite reel of the most memorable tosses. Some of them went to U.S. Senator Bob Kerrey, a former pharmacy college colleague. Kerrey often sat in the West Stadium, around the 40-yard line, maybe 20-25 rows deep. Depending on the wind, it could be a tricky throw. The senator wasn't a great leaper, recalls Potter, "yet he always seemed to jump a little higher when he brought Debra Winger to the game.

"But Bob had decent hands — and he was a competitor. If the throw was anywhere close, he'd go for it. He wanted the completion and so did I. Completions are very important."

Asked to identify his most memorable completion, Potter doesn't hesitate. It was the autumn of 1994. East Stadium. Exceptionally windy. A very large man, perhaps 300 pounds, dressed in bib overalls, seated maybe 30 rows up, signaled for the 'dog. He had to throw it straight overhand that day, faster than usual, as hard as he could. "The wind caught it about half-way up and it started to sail on me. But the man stretched as high as he could and went for it. And then he toppled over backwards and his two legs shot straight up in the air. From where I was standing, they looked like goal posts."

A hush fell over the section. And then, after a few moments, there came a mighty roar. "I saw his arm come up out of the mass of bodies, just a single arm, and it had the 'dog in it.

"When he fell, he had wedged himself into the seats and it took four others to unwedge him. But he eventually got back up and he had the 'dog. He never dropped it. I don't think I'll ever be able to top that one."

Only in Nebraska, perhaps, could there be a serious debate as to whether the hotdog vendor possesses a better arm than some of the quarterbacks.

No matter how strong his arm, the hotdog man can't reach **Carl W. Olson**. That's because Carl now sits in the glassed-in press box high atop the West Stadium. It seems appropriate. After all, his construction company built the facility and it affords him a fine view of Nebraska home football games, something of a life-long pursuit. And the term "life-long" is not used lightly here.

He was at Memorial Stadium in the fall of 1995 to see the Nebraska-Arizona State game. In fact, Carl Olson saw his first Nebraska football game four years after Arizona was admitted to the Union and four years before American women could vote. A year before the Bolshevik Revolution. A year before the U.S. entered World War I. The same year John J. Pershing went off to Mexico in search of Pancho Villa. The year Carl Olson saw his first Nebraska home game Woodrow Wilson was in the White House.

It was the autumn of 1916.

He was 11 years old and, in a big upset, he saw Kansas beat Nebraska in Lincoln that fall. It made a lasting impression. Nine years later, as a University of Nebraska freshmen, he saw all of the 1925 home football games. And he saw them all in 1926 and 1927. In 1928, his senior year, he was an Innocents Society member in charge of the student rooting section. He saw all the home games that year, too. In fact, from September 1925 to November 1995, Carl Olson saw every Nebraska home football game.

"There was a game sometime in the 50s that I was late for," says Olson, somewhat apologetically. "I had to go to a funeral in Omaha and I didn't get there until the second half. But that's it."

Until recently, he estimates he's also seen about 90 percent of all the away games. He and friends would fly to road games in a private plane. "Our pilot died about three or four years ago and then some of my other buddies died. There's nobody left to go with anymore. And my legs have kind of given out, anyway. I can't do that climb up the hill in Lawrence anymore."

But those are road games. At 90, he can still get to all the home games, even if it takes crutches now to get up the steps to get to the elevator to get to the press box atop Memorial Stadium.

The son of the founder of Olson Construction Company, he quite easily recalls games, scores and plays from half-a-century ago. Each decade of Nebraska football brings the memories. He remembers his nephew, Bobby Reynolds, lighting up Memorial Stadium in the 50s, Bill "Thunder" Thornton and Ben Gregory in the 60s, Johnny Rodgers and Jerry Tagge in the 70s, the Turner Gill-Mike Rozier-Irving Fryar teams of the 80s, and Trev Alberts, Tommie Frazier and Lawrence Phillips in the 90s.

Can he take it to another century?

"I've got bad legs and a bad back now. When I go out, I need crutches and when I'm home, it's mostly in a wheelchair. But I know I'm happiest in the fall. It's good weather and the football season starts.

"It's the best time of year."

The game is winding down, almost over, and it doesn't seem quite possible, but this is Nebraska and this is football and there does happen to be another fan who understands autumn like Carl Olson, who understands what it's like to see a game late in the fourth quarter.

His name is **Wayne Ballah**.

In an age in which it is not unusual to switch jobs, switch homes, switch spouses and switch allegiances on a whim, Wayne is something of a throwback. He has lived in the same neighborhood in the same community for 55 years, has worked at the same company for 69 years and has passionately followed Nebraska football for 80 years. The same college football team he once played for — in 1922.

Wayne Ballah is 93.

Born January 25, 1903, in Neligh, Nebraska, he and his family later moved to Cambridge, where Wayne played on the school's 1920 state champion football team. Five years earlier, he had gone to Lincoln for an operation. That fall — 1915 — an older brother took him to his first college football game. The 12-year-old boy saw Nebraska beat Notre Dame — 20 to 19 — and he has been a dyed-in-the-wool Husker ever since.

In 1922, Ballah joined the Nebraska football team as a walk-on. "Back then," he says, "almost everyone was a walk-on and we just played for fun." He also made another contribution to the program that year: He donated $100 to help build a new stadium — Memorial Stadium.

The following year, 1923, he again went out for the team, playing a little quarterback and left halfback. He didn't make the traveling squad, however, so for the first game that year — an away game — he initiated what would later become a routine habit: Ballah got behind the wheel of a Model T Ford and drove from Lincoln to Champaign, Illinois. There, he rooted for his team to beat the Fighting Illini, who were showcasing their star running back for the first time. Fellow named Red Grange. Alas, Grange & Co. were too much and the Huskers lost 24-7. But a week later, on Oct. 13, 1923, Ballah and his teammates returned to Lincoln and beat Oklahoma 24-0. He remembers the day well: It was the first game ever played at Memorial Stadium. And the next year, 1924, Ballah and his Husker mates beat Red Grange and Illinois in Lincoln.

The day after Wayne Ballah graduated from the University of Nebraska in 1927, he went to work for the Northwestern Mutual Life Insurance Company in Norfolk. He's still with the company. Only now, it's in Fort Collins, Colorado, his home since 1941. The 93-year-old insurance agent is usually in his office by 8 a.m., making calls, returning calls, fine-tuning his clients' needs, sitting at a tidy desk not far from a framed 1923 photo of the Nebraska football team. In 1995, he was one of 19 agents (out of 9,000 nationwide) cited by the company "for outstanding community service."

And there's the rub.

Although Wayne was recognized for his devotion to the Colorado community, it pales compared to his investment in a neighboring state to the east.

Since 1987, two years after his wife died, Ballah has driven from Fort Collins to Lincoln for every home football game. The routine never varies. He leaves Fort Collins precisely at 7 a.m. Friday, driving alone, dressed in red, in a Mercedes sporting a Nebraska helmet, a 1992 autographed Nebraska football and a "1994 Huskers National Champions" sign — all conveniently displayed in the rear window. He arrives in Kearney at 4 p.m., spending the night with a sister-in-law, a brother-in-law and a niece. Saturday morning, he squires the three relatives to the University Club for lunch, then to the game, then back to Kearney afterwards. After church on Sunday morning, he again sets off alone, and by evening — three days and a thousand miles later — he's back in Fort Collins. And in the office by 8 a.m. Monday.

A creature of habit, he strictly adheres to a number of time-honored rituals. One begins each summer. Wherever he goes in Fort Collins, whether gardening, grocery shopping, running to

the bank or the post office, he makes sure he's wearing his trademark red-and-white Nebraska football hat. "I start getting mentally prepared about June and the cap helps. It helps get me in the right mood for fall."

He was in a particularly good mood throughout the fall of 1995. "I'll tell you, that Frazier is something. Everywhere you look, the amount of talent they have is unreal.

"I think," he said, "it may be the best Nebraska team I've ever seen."

In various writing circles, this would be called "perspective." That is to say, at 105, the Nebraska football program has only been around a dozen years longer than Wayne.

Asked the secret to a long and healthy life, Ballah answers without a hint of hyperbole. A quick, two-word response: "Nebraska Football."

"I just can't stand the thought of not being in the stadium on Saturdays. Of not being around for the start of another season. It scares me to, well — I won't say to death — but it does scare me."

The game is over now and the late autumn sunlight begins to fade. Down on the field, some of the players mingle easily with some of the children, taking them in their arms, taking their autograph requests, taking care of the next generation of fans. High above, in the upper deck of the East Stadium, an older fan sits alone, lost in his headphones, staring at the field below. Outside, a father and son lay sprawled on the steps. They are playful, relaxed, content to idle away the time until their ride appears. Tens of thousands of others are flowing through the gates, back across campus, to the parking lots, to the RVs and vans and station wagons and pickups, to the Haymarket and *Barry's* and the Cornhusker Hotel, to their homes in Weeping Water, David City, Rulo and Ravenna.

◔ 5:30 PM

Everyone has left. Inside, it is still and empty. Outside, the sun silently slips toward the horizon of the western shortgrass prairie and soon the late autumn evening gives way to floodlights. Amid the gathering dusk, a fading patch of sunlight briefly illuminates one small corner of Memorial Stadium, until only the words remain:

NOT THE VICTORY BUT THE ACTION. NOT THE GOAL BUT THE GAME. IN THE DEED THE GLORY.

About the Author

Joe Starita was an award-winning veteran investigative journalist before he moved back to his hometown of Lincoln, Nebraska in 1992. Among the stories Mr. Starita covered were the Bernhard Goetz subway shooting, the space shuttle Challenger explosion, the Los Angeles Summer Olympics, and the downfall of 1988 presidential candidate Gary Hart. Since moving back to Nebraska, he has completed work on a three-year project about Native Americans on the Pine Ridge Reservation, culminating in his first book. *The Dull Knifes of Pine Ridge* (G.P. Putnam's Sons/New York) has earned Mr. Starita a nomination for the Pulitzer Prize.

About the Photographer

Tom Tidball left his hometown of Lincoln, Nebraska in 1971 to pursue a career in photography. He has traveled and worked extensively in Southeast Asia. Mr. Tidball's unique photographic perspective has graced numerous travel guides and periodicals, including science and performing arts magazines. His work is regularly sought for publication by international airlines and commercial advertising agencies worldwide. Thousands of Big Red fans have hung his posters in offices, lobbies, dorm rooms and homes across the nation. Previous books featuring Mr. Tidball's photographs include *Sri Lanka* and *The University of Nebraska - A Timeless Experience*.

Designer: Elizabeth Bannetine

Printer: Jacob North Printing Company

Color Separations: Lincoln Graphics

Publisher: Nebraska Book Publishing Company
1300 Q Street ~ Lincoln, Nebraska 68508
Phone: 800-627-0027
402-476-7755
Fax: 402-476-0111
E-Mail: nbookstore@aol.com

Thanks to the UNL Archives and UNL Publications and Photography for archival photographs.

Printed and Produced in Lincoln, Nebraska U.S.A.